MASADA

Written and Illustrated by

Neil Waldman

MORROW JUNIOR BOOKS ✦ *New York*

To the men of my sacred circle—Alan Goncharoff, Tom Schaeffer, Paul McGregor, Myron Zackman, John Hickok, Andy Liebman, Mark Liebman, and Marc Broxmeyer

Thanks to my editor, Meredith Charpentier, who crafted this ambitious project with inspired insight, sensitivity, and vision; to Claire Counihan, whose wonderful sense of design graces the book's pages; and to Rabbi Mark Dov Shapiro for his expert counsel in the shaping of the manuscript.

Acrylics and india ink were used for the illustrations.
The text type is 14-point Plantin Light.

Published by Morrow Junior Books
a division of William Morrow and Company, Inc.
1350 Avenue of the Americas, New York, NY 10019
www.williammorrow.com

Printed in Singapore at Tien Wah Press.

10 9 8 7 6 5 4 3 2 1

Library of Congress Cataloging-in-Publication Data
Waldman, Neil.
Masada/Neil Waldman.
p. cm.
Includes bibliographical references and index.
Summary: Discusses the history of Masada, from the building of Herod's Temple through its use by Zealots as a refuge from the Romans to its excavation in the mid-20th century.
ISBN 0-688-14481-0
1. Masada Site (Israel)—Siege, 72–73—Juvenile literature.   2. Jews—History—Rebellion, 66–73—Juvenile literature.   3. Excavations (Archaeology)—Israel—Masada Site—Juvenile literature.   [1. Masada Site (Israel).   2. Jews—History—Rebellion, 66–73.   3. Excavations (Archaeology)—Israel—Masada Site.]   I. Title.
DS110.M33W35 1998   933—dc21   97-32912   CIP AC

Contents

IN THE CHILLY DESERT NIGHT, I slowly made my way up the side of the sheer cliff. The sky was spectacular, like a black velvet sea filled with sparkling diamonds. But I rarely glanced up, for the narrow path that snaked its way up Masada's eastern wall required every bit of my concentration. When I reached the top, I sat on the defense wall while the sky lightened and the sun peeked over the mountains of Jordan.

In the desert far below, the parking lots slowly filled with cars, buses, and vans. Long lines of tourists waited for the cable car that would carry them to the top of the fabled plateau. A group of Israeli soldiers passed through the ancient wall of a Roman army camp and began their ascent up the Snake Path.

Masada has become a very important symbol of heroism to the people of the Jewish state. Israeli children are required to study the history of the fortress in school. Units of the army perform their induction ceremony at the summit, swearing an oath of allegiance to their country. Thousands of Israelis drive into the desert each year to explore the ruins of the legendary citadel.

With a legacy of unending wars, Israel has spent most of the twentieth century surrounded by large and hostile armies, just like the Zealots of Masada. It is no wonder that the words *Masada shall not fall again!* can be found anywhere from postage stamps and medallions to the blackboards of high school classrooms.

THE
ROMAN
EMPIRE
218 B.C.E.
to 100 C.E.

BRITANNIA

GALLIA

ITALIA

Rome

HISPANIA

AFRICA

MAURETANIA

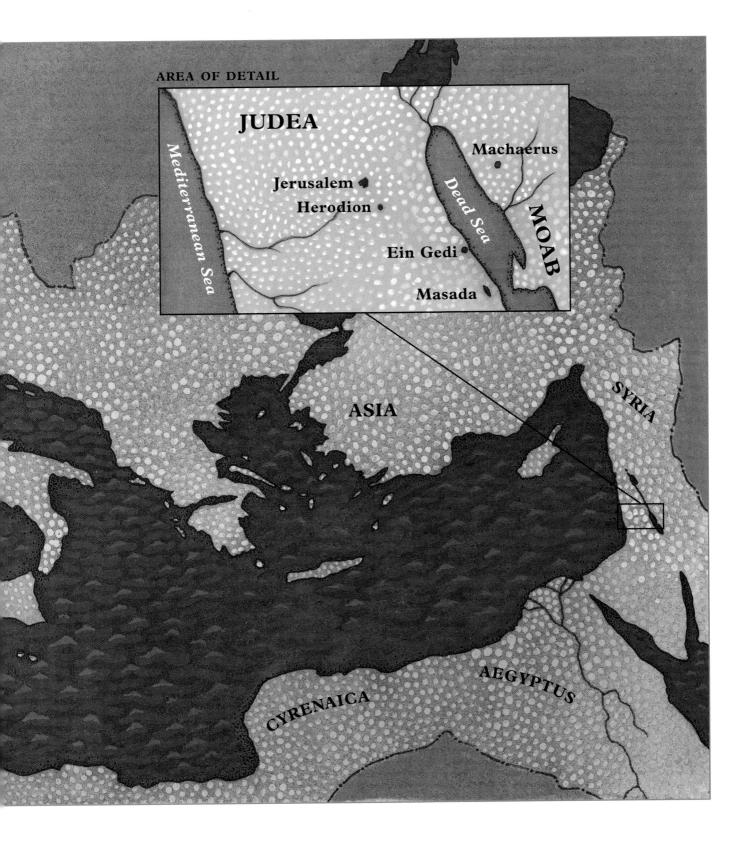

AREA OF DETAIL

JUDEA

Mediterranean Sea

Jerusalem
Herodion

Machaerus

Dead Sea

MOAB

Ein Gedi

Masada

ASIA

SYRIA

CYRENAICA

AEGYPTUS

Jerusalem—66 C.E.

IN THE TERRIBLE HEAT of a midsummer afternoon, several hundred wooden crosses lined the sides of the eastern road that led from the city walls down into the valley of Jericho. On each cross, a man hung suspended, dying slowly beneath the oppressive sun. Roman guards gripping swords in their right hands stood at attention along the roadside, with orders not to allow anyone to give the dying men even the smallest drink of water.

It had all started when Gessius Florus, the Roman governor, sent a small company of centurions into the Holy Temple, where they seized a portion of the Temple treasure. Florus announced that the action was taken to reclaim unpaid taxes owed to Rome. But the local people were not so gullible. They knew that Florus was in terrible financial trouble and had appropriated the money for his own personal needs.

Following the seizure, a group of outraged Jews circulated in the marketplace, carrying woven baskets, sarcastically begging for donations of copper coins for their "impoverished" ruler. Infuriated by the public mockery, Florus sent several units of infantry and cavalry into the crowded marketplace with orders to kill all the Jews they could find. The highly trained troops rushed in and cornered hundreds of screaming people in the narrow alleyways. The soldiers thrust wildly with their short Roman swords until their arms were so weary that they could no longer lift them. In the end, six hundred men, women, and children lay dead. Those men who survived the slaughter were brutally whipped and then crucified beyond the city walls.

A great outcry echoed through the countryside. A rebellion erupted from the northern borders of Galilee to the Judean wilderness in the south. Farmers and fishermen, merchants and musicians, poets and scholars armed themselves and joined forces in a massive effort to throw the Roman occupiers from their bloodstained homeland.

The first place to fall to the Jews was the fortress of Masada. This spectacular citadel had been designed a century earlier by a demented genius named Herod, a brilliant ruler who built many magnificent cities throughout Judea. But Herod was also an extremely insecure man. He was terrified that his family and friends were plotting to kill him, suspicious that the Romans had plans to remove him from the throne. And so he built several fortresses for himself, to escape to in times of danger. Masada was one such place.

As a young man, Herod had fled there with eight hundred of his followers during one of the frequent Jewish revolts against Rome. He remained on the plateau for several months and was impressed with its potential as a stronghold. After he was crowned king, Herod embarked on a massive building program to strengthen the natural fortress in the wilderness.

He constructed a thick defense wall upon the sheer cliffs, enclosing the entire top of the plateau. Inside this wall, he built a luxurious city of villas and palaces, complete with all the comforts of a royal residence. An ingenious system of underground reservoirs was carved into the bedrock of Masada. It was designed to collect rainwater from the surrounding area during the rare flash floods that raged through the desert once or twice a year. Herod also built barracks for a large army and storehouses of weapons, enough to withstand a long siege. There were other storehouses filled with preserved foods of many kinds, including Herod's personal wine from the vineyards of Italy.

As Herod grew older, he became progressively more insane. Terrors consumed him, and he began killing those he feared. He drowned his brother-in-law. He had two of his sons strangled and another drowned. Finally, he ordered the execution of his beloved wife, the beautiful princess Mariamme. He stumbled aimlessly about the palace in a state of perpetual torment, unbathed and unsightly, wildly shrieking at the ghosts of those he'd murdered. In the end, he died a slow and excruciating death from stomach cancer, tortured by the unbearable pain that continued unrelenting through his final days and nights. He never returned to Masada.

After Herod's death, the country quickly descended into a time of chaos. An earthquake destroyed many of the beautiful towns that Herod had built. Several years later, a prolonged drought resulted in famine. Bands of desperate, hungry people wandered through the hillsides, following self-proclaimed prophets who preached that the Messiah would arrive as soon as the Romans were overthrown.

As the decades passed, the country teetered on the brink of war. A series of oppressive and incompetent Roman governors further galvanized the local population. In the northern province of Galilee, people began rallying behind a group called the Zealots, who had long called for open rebellion against the Roman occupiers. Their numbers swelled into the thousands, and they began preparing to attack. In the deserts of the south, a fierce group of Zealots known as the Sicarii, or "Daggermen," started killing all those who refused to join in their campaign to drench the land with Roman blood.

Masada, the Judean Wilderness—66 C.E.

O N A MOONLESS DESERT NIGHT, a curving line of Sicarii crept silently up Masada's eastern cliffs. For hours, they inched onward, careful not to dislodge even a single pebble. As they neared the summit, they could see a sleeping Roman guard slouched on a stone bench within the gatehouse. The lead climber motioned for the others to halt and, with the fluid movements of a cat, approached the Roman alone. Sliding up behind his unsuspecting victim, he slowly drew a long curved dagger from his belt. Then he pounced. There was a flash of silver and it was over. Crouching motionless for several seconds, the daggerman slowly guided the lifeless body down onto the ground. He beckoned silently to the others, and one by one they slipped through the gate and into the fortress.

Within a short time, Masada was theirs. Most of the small Roman garrison were killed in their beds, and the few who managed to grab their swords did not last much longer. As the morning sun rose over the mountains of Moab, the triumphant blast of a ram's horn sounded from the walls of the fortress.

Moments later, the blast of a second horn answered from the desert below. The men in the lofty fortress looked down as their wives and children emerged from a hidden wadi and began ascending the narrow Snake Path.

When the local Roman rulers learned of the outbreak of hostilities, they rushed three thousand cavalrymen to Jerusalem to protect the

Roman garrison there. They were quickly outnumbered by waves of Jewish militiamen who poured into the Holy City from surrounding farms and villages. After several days of bloody fighting in the streets, the beleaguered Romans offered to surrender. They asked only that they be allowed to leave the country. The Jewish officers agreed. But when the Romans walked out into the open and laid down their arms, they were slaughtered by the frenzied Jewish mob.

The revolt spread quickly through the country, and within months the entire Roman occupation force had been decimated. After the victory celebrations, the Jews reorganized their militia and repaired their fortresses, brashly awaiting the Roman response.

In Rome, the emperor Nero learned of his army's defeat. He realized that he couldn't allow such a tiny nation to stand up against the might of Rome. And so Nero decided to send a clear message to all the conquered peoples of the empire: Any rebellion, no matter how small, would be crushed speedily and without mercy. He chose the great general Vespasian to lead a massive army eastward into Judea.

Nero

As Vespasian's army passed through Syria, he was met by his son Titus, leading the powerful fifteenth legion. They were joined by several armies from neighboring allies. Together they descended into Israel and stormed into the northern province of Galilee. City after city was surrounded and crushed.

Then they began to march southward toward Jerusalem. More than a million Jews had flocked there from all over the country, and they readied themselves to defend their Holy City to the bitter end. But in Rome, the emperor died. A bloody civil war erupted, and Vespasian hastened home. For many months, the Roman army sat on the hillsides beyond Jerusalem's walls, waiting for orders to attack. After a prolonged power struggle, Vespasian was crowned emperor and his son Titus assumed command. Within days, the Roman army descended upon the city.

Titus knew that the Jews had a meager supply of food and water, and he decided to break their fighting spirit in a slow and methodical manner. He ordered his troops to build a circumvallation wall to cut off any routes of escape for the beleaguered Jews.

A tall slender man wearing the clothes of a Roman civilian stepped inside the outer wall and began calling out to the defenders of the city.

"Dear fellow Jews," he shouted, "I am here to offer you the opportunity to surrender honorably. If you will renounce your foolish ways and become Roman, as I have, we are prepared to spare your lives."

From the city ramparts, the Jews stared in disbelief, for many recognized this famous man. He was Yosef Ben Matitiahu, one of their most promising young leaders. He had commanded the Jewish forces of Galilee, and it was assumed that he had died in the battle for the walled city of Jotapata. But unknown to these Judeans, he had hidden in a cave with forty others as the Romans broke through the walls. After failing to persuade his comrades to surrender, he convinced them to take their own lives. When the others had done so, he walked out into the open and swore allegiance to the Roman side.

"This is your last opportunity to survive the coming days," he called out again. "Please, save your own lives while you still can!"

A young Zealot captain with a thick reddish beard stood up and yelled from the wall, "Yosef, what are you doing? You are not a Roman! Do you not remember that we fought side by side in the north?"

"Of course I remember," the tall man answered. "But listen to me,

Eleazar. I am presenting you with the opportunity to save your lives! Right now, that's all that matters!"

"God forgive you, Yosef," the young Zealot called back.

"My name is no longer Yosef!" the tall man screamed out in anger. "I am now called Josephus Flavius!"

The people of Jerusalem were infuriated. Shouts of "Traitor!" rang from the walls, followed by a volley of arrows, spears, and stones.

Josephus Flavius turned to run for cover, and an arrow struck him in the thigh. He fell to the ground and dragged himself behind the protection of the outer wall.

Several weeks passed. Food and water disappeared, and the streets of the city were piled with the bodies of the dead and dying. Titus ordered a total assault, and the last surviving Jews were too weak to resist. The Romans broke through the ramparts, and wave after wave of centurions poured into the city.

Sixty thousand Jews retreated to the Temple compound and prepared to make a last desperate stand. They stood upon the walls that surrounded the outer courtyard of the Temple and struggled against the onslaught of Romans, who climbed toward them on long wooden ladders. For several days, they managed to withstand repeated attacks. But then the Temple itself caught fire, and a rising tide of flame reached upward into the sky. In the intense heat, the metal of the massive doors melted, and a fiery pool of molten brass began spilling down the steps.

A group of warriors and their families made their way past the burning temple to an ancient underground passageway that led to the Gihon spring, beyond the city walls. They were led by the red-bearded Zealot captain, Eleazar Ben Yair. Among them was a rabbi carrying a sacred Torah scroll.

In the dark of night, they crept out into the Valley of Kidron. A pale pink glow slowly filled the eastern sky as they made their way through a grove of ancient olive trees, descending steadily downward through the valley toward the fortress of Masada.

THREE

Rome—70 C.E.

A s Eleazar Ben Yair and his group of Zealots reached Masada, Jerusalem was reduced to a smoldering heap of rubble by the conquering Romans. Only three isolated fortresses were still in Jewish hands, and the bulk of the Roman army returned to their capital for the traditional victory celebrations. A small force stayed on to maintain order and to clean up the few remaining pockets of Jewish resistance.

General Titus made his way to Egypt, from where he set sail for Italy. As he stepped onto the shore of his native land, his father, the emperor Vespasian, greeted him warmly. A large crowd had gathered for the occasion, and they cheered in approval, enthusiastically welcoming Titus back home.

Several days later, the citizens of Rome flocked to the streets to witness the spectacular victory celebrations. Vespasian and Titus, wearing bay wreaths and traditional crimson robes, emerged from the emperor's palace and proceeded to the Portico of Octavia. On chairs of ivory, they sat upon a golden dais that had been specially constructed for the occasion.

From within the Temple of Isis, long lines of centurions marched in formation, led by their commanders. They halted in front of the emperor and his son and shouted out praises and accolades to their victorious general. Then Vespasian gave the signal for silence. A hush fell over the masses as the emperor rose from his chair, draped his cloak over his head, and offered prayers to the Roman gods. Titus rose and

Vespasian congratulated the general and his troops for their great triumph. The soldiers were then dismissed for a traditional victory breakfast and sacrifices to the gods.

At midday, they returned to the streets for the triumphal procession. A wide variety of animals pulling magnificent displays of wealth and beauty were led past the crowd. Treasures from many conquered nations of the empire were exhibited in all their splendor. There were portraits in bright colors by the Babylonian masters, and golden crowns studded with huge gems. Alongside these displays marched Roman escorts dressed in bright purple robes trimmed with gold.

But what caused the greatest sensation were the massive constructions that passed the crowd on ornately carved stages. Three and four stories high, they depicted scenes from the recent war. Many were hung with curtains of woven gold, framed in iron and silver with gold and ivory decorations. A Roman commander stood on each stage before a dramatic depiction of the town or city he had captured. These were rendered in tableau style, with an array of men in Roman and Judean costume frozen in the heat of battle. The entire story of the war was thus shown, from Vespasian's arrival in Galilee to the destruction of the Holy Temple in Jerusalem. It served as a newsreel, informing the people of the historic events that had just taken place.

The tableaux were followed by great collections of the spoils of war, including many precious objects that had been taken from the Holy Temple. Among them were a great golden table, a colossal seven-branched menorah, and several sacred Torah scrolls. Next came long

Vespasian

lines of captured Jewish warriors under heavy guard, led by their commander, Simon Bar Giora. As they were paraded through the streets, people in the crowd shouted insults and curses at them.

Titus

They were followed by many images of the Roman gods of victory, carved in gold and ivory. At the rear of the procession, Vespasian and Titus galloped by on chariots of gold pulled by magnificent white stallions. They stopped before the Temple of Jupiter and waited for news that the enemy commander in chief was dead.

A group of Roman guards approached Simon Bar Giora, who had been marching at the head of the Jewish prisoners. They bound his hands behind his back and placed a noose around his neck. A centurion on horseback took the rope and began pulling him through the streets. At first, he ran behind the prancing horse, but soon the horse began to gallop. Simon lost his balance and fell. He twisted and bounced on the cobblestones as the centurion dragged him onward, slowly choking him to death. His limp and broken body was brought to the spot on the Forum reserved for those who had committed crimes against the state.

News of Simon's death was passed on to Vespasian and Titus, and a thunderous cheer erupted from the massive crowd. The emperor then recited the customary prayers, and the ceremonies ended.

Vespasian and Titus retired to the emperor's palace, where they entertained a host of royal dignitaries in a series of sumptuous feasts that lasted for days.

Masada—71 C.E.

FTER THE FALL OF JERUSALEM, a steady stream of refugees began to arrive at the desert fortress. Traveling by night to avoid capture by the Romans, they had spent the daylight hours hiding in caves and wadis. Many reached Masada thirsty and wounded, having barely survived the terrible slaughter they had witnessed.

Most of the warriors came from families who had been fighting against the Romans for many years. They had lived in hiding, never knowing the warmth of a fireplace in winter or the comforts of their own beds.

But now, for the first time in their lives, they settled into a routine. Three times a day they filled the synagogue with chanting and prayers to their God. The rabbi held regular classes in the study of Torah, and the synagogue was barely large enough to hold the overflowing crowds that attended. For many, this was their first opportunity to practice the commandments Moses had brought down from Mount Sinai. The Zealots partook of them fully and happily.

Refugees continued arriving at Masada, and their numbers swelled to nine hundred sixty men, women, and children. At one of their weekly meetings, the people chose Eleazar Ben Yair to be their commander. He led with a calm and steady hand and instilled in the people feelings of confidence in the future. But then, on a hot and windy afternoon, a family reached Masada from Machaerus, another Jewish stronghold. They brought grim news that both their town and the fortress of Herodion had been taken by the Romans. Masada now stood alone.

As the sun rose on a cloudless desert morning, a sentry standing high in a watchtower spotted a small red cloud of dust on the northern horizon. The cloud grew steadily larger, and tiny sparkles appeared within it, like distant stars.

People began stirring within the fortress. The quiet chanting of morning prayers drifted up from the synagogue. A second sentry climbed up into the watchtower, about to begin his daily shift. He approached his fellow watchman, who stood frozen, still staring out into the desert.

"What is it?" the replacement asked, his worried eyes suddenly widening.

"I don't know," came the quick answer.

The replacement leaned over the stone wall of the tower, straining to identify the source of the dust cloud.

"How long has it been out there?" he asked.

"Since sunrise."

The ominous cloud moved slowly closer, rising above the flatlands along the shoreline of the Dead Sea. Its movement was almost imperceptible. But as it rose ever so slowly from the crest of a distant hill, rows of tiny specks came into view. It was soon clear that they were soldiers, with sparkles glinting from their helmets.

The walls of Masada slowly filled with people who watched in silence as the distant army drew steadily nearer. It was led by a company of cavalrymen holding square red banners high above them. For hours, they continued onward, over hills and across dried riverbeds, approaching through the desolate wilderness. By late afternoon, the lead riders had reached the valley floor near the base of the plateau. Just below the horizon, the tiny specks continued marching over the crest of the distant hill. The sun set behind the western mountains, and endless lines of soldiers sliced through the purple shadows of the desert. When night finally fell, a force of twenty thousand stood at the base of Masada.

Commander Eleazar Ben Yair called the men to a war council in the western palace. He met each man at the door with a warm handshake or a tug on the shoulders. When they had all arrived, he climbed several steps on the broad stairway behind him.

"My dear friends," he began. "When we left Jerusalem, I vowed to the rabbi that our Torah would never fall into Roman hands. I knew that there was just one place in all of Israel that they could never take. It was a fortress so high and mighty that all the legions of all the empires would be hard-pressed to conquer it."

He looked across at their weathered faces and he could see that his words had begun to rouse them.

"And after six years of war," he continued, "there is only one fortress they have failed to conquer."

"Masada!" yelled one of the Sicarii, as he thrust a fist in the air.

"Masada!" echoed other voices from across the hall.

Commander Ben Yair waited for a moment, and the room became quiet again.

"Soon the Romans will try to scale the cliffs," he proclaimed. "But God will never allow them to succeed. Neither will the boulders that we roll down upon them. Those that make such foolhardy attempts will be crushed to death. . . . And when they begin to lose heart, we'll descend by night and slowly crush their spirit with our daggers!"

The following morning, Commander Flavius Silva slowly circled the base of the plateau. Riding a black stallion, he stopped often and spoke to his scribe, who wrote his comments on a scroll of parchment. After several hours, Silva completed the circle and returned to his tent.

The attack began two days later. Long lines of Roman soldiers in full battle gear began simultaneously climbing the eastern and western sides of Masada. They made their way slowly up the steep cliffs, glancing occasionally at the walls of the fortress high above them. The Jews waited patiently as the Romans steadily approached. Then, at Eleazar's command, they began rolling boulders down from the cliffs. The Romans stopped and raised their shields above their heads, trying in vain to protect themselves. The heavy boulders came tumbling down toward them, dislodging hundreds of stones as they fell. The landslide poured over the Romans, knocking many to their deaths in the valley below.

The Romans tried the same tactics on the following night, hoping that they might go undetected in the darkness. But the Jewish sentries spotted them, and the desert floor was again littered with corpses. For several days, the Romans attempted to reach the fortress, but the results remained the same. They soon grew disheartened. Not one of their soldiers had reached Masada's walls.

Commander Ben Yair approached one of the Sicarii.

"Select five of your best warriors," he said. "After the moon sets tonight, slip down into six Roman campsites and slit the throat of one soldier in each."

And so it was done. Six of the Sicarii silently descended into the Roman tents, killed six enemy soldiers in their sleep, and returned to the fortress before sunrise. Panic swept through the Roman ranks.

Three days later, the Sicarii descended once again, killing six others in six different tents. When the Romans awoke in the morning and discovered their slain comrades lying upon pillows soaked in blood, they were profoundly shaken. And so Commander Silva directed hundreds of Jewish slaves to build a circumvallation wall around the entire base of the plateau, in order to protect his troops and prevent the Jews from escaping. After several weeks, the wall was completed. The Romans posted guards upon it, and the night raids came to an end.

The Ramp, Masada—73 C.E.

IN THE COOL SHADOWS just before dawn, hundreds of slaves marched out toward the western side of Masada. Beneath the whips of their Roman masters, they began carting rocks and earth to the base of the plateau. Piling them in a large triangular area, they worked through the day as sentries stared down from their towers. The Zealots soon realized that the Romans were constructing a ramp in order to haul their giant war machines up to the defense wall and attack the fortress.

In the coming months, the pile of rocks and earth rose steadily higher and higher. It had nearly reached the halfway point, and Commander Ben Yair couldn't devise a way to stop it. The Romans had positioned a huge assault tower at the base of the ramp and placed catapults and archers upon its highest platforms. When the Zealots appeared on the walls, they were greeted with a barrage of stones, arrows, and spears. A heavy sense of foreboding hung over the fortress.

A month later, the ramp reached the base of the wall, more than three hundred feet above the desert floor. With huge pulleys, the slaves began hauling large cubes of rock up the long incline. Upon the top of the ramp, they constructed a square platform seventy-five feet wide. They then attached the massive assault tower to the pulleys and began hauling it up the ramp. Beneath the sting of Roman whips, the slaves slowly dragged the huge tower into position and anchored it to the platform.

Within the tower, a log as big as the mast of a great ship hung suspended from a network of ropes. Looming on the front of the log was the colossal iron head of a ram.

That evening, Commander Flavius Silva ascended the ramp with a group of his officers. They climbed up into the assault tower and, from the highest platform, looked down into Masada. Silva peered across the sloping tile roof of the western palace, scanning the empty streets and alleyways of the citadel.

"What a magnificent place," he remarked.

"Yes," agreed one of the officers. "It certainly is."

Silva smiled. "By this time tomorrow," he said, "it will be ours."

The final assault began as the sun rose over the mountains of Moab. An unrelenting torrent of spears and stones ricocheted across the fortress as scores of Zealots ran for cover in the western palace. Within the assault tower, a team of slaves pulled on the network of ropes and let go. The mighty battering ram swung in a great arc, crashing into Masada's defense wall. With a sound like the booming of thunder, the earth trembled and several large stones fell to the ground. Again and again, the ram smashed into the wall until a jagged crack appeared. Within the tower and on the ramp, long lines of Roman soldiers tensed, awaiting the final charge.

Commander Ben Yair and a large group of Zealots raced through the storm of flying arrows to the defense wall, carrying picks and shovels. As the earth continued shaking beneath the heavy blows of the ram, they dug two deep trenches just inside the wall, an arm's width apart. A second group arrived, carrying long, heavy wooden beams.

"Lay the beams lengthwise within the trenches!" Eleazar yelled. "And pile them high, one upon the other. Join them at both ends with vertical beams."

The men began working feverishly. Several were struck down by Roman arrows, but in a short time two wooden walls stood just inside the crumbling defense wall. They grabbed shovels and frantically filled the narrow space between the wooden walls with earth. Moments later, a jagged section of the defense wall teetered and came tumbling down.

The Zealots ran, exhausted, to the protection of the western palace. They peered through the windows as the Romans repositioned the ram. Within minutes, the pounding resumed. With each blow, muffled thuds rumbled across the plateau. The wood gave way a bit, compressing the earth between the wooden walls and making the new wall stronger. As the sun rose slowly in the eastern sky, the steady pounding continued until Commander Silva realized that the mighty battering ram had been rendered useless. From the highest platform of the assault tower, he gave the order to halt.

Within the palace, the Zealots stared at each other in disbelief. They listened intently for the heavy blows of the ram to resume, but there was silence. Then, suddenly, a torrent of flaming arrows filled the skies. Like a rain of fire, the arrows streaked downward in great arcs, striking the wooden wall again and again. A rising sea of flame leaped from the burning beams and soared upward into the sky.

Ben Yair commanded his people to form lines from the cisterns to the wooden wall. Men and women began filling large clay jugs with water. But a strong southern wind blew scorching flames into the faces of those near the wall, and they couldn't get close enough to douse the blaze. They tried again and again to approach the wall, but the heat was unbearable. Finally, they fell exhausted on the ground, realizing that all their efforts had been in vain. Their wooden wall had only one weakness and the Romans had discovered it.

Just then, strong gusts of wind from the north blew over Masada. The weary Zealots felt the cool air on their blackened brows. The gusts grew even stronger, blowing past them and into the roaring fire. One by one, the exhausted warriors stood up and faced the wind.

A young sentry made his way up onto the roof of the palace. He cupped his hands over his mouth and began to yell.

"The wind is destroying the Romans!" he cried. The others soon joined him on the roof and looked on silently as long waves of fire pounded the giant assault tower and the battering ram. Swarms of frenzied Romans fled from the tower and rushed down the ramp, trying desperately to escape the swirling flames.

The astonished men and women stared in wonder as the flames

engulfed the massive war machines. The rabbi raised his head and gazed up into the heavens.

"Baruch Ata Adonai . . . ," he began. "Blessed are You, O Lord our God. . . ."

Soon they were all chanting together, their joyful prayer reaching upward into the evening sky.

But suddenly the north wind hushed. For an eternity of heartbeats, a deathly stillness hung in the air. The people stood frozen on the palace roof and the air began to stir once again. Moments later, a strong wind began to blow, but this time it didn't come from the north. Now it gusted from the opposite direction. The flames leaped away from the Roman war machines, turning once again upon the Zealots of Masada. Suddenly surrounded by a cloud of swirling black smoke, the Zealots fled from the roof as Roman soldiers came charging back up the ramp. They all stood watching as the wooden wall was slowly devoured by the crackling fire.

Night fell over Masada, and the Romans returned down the ramp. A burly centurion looked back through the flames at the weary Jewish warriors.

"Sleep well!" he jeered. "We'll see you in the morning."

The Western Palace, Masada—73 C.E.

ELEAZAR BEN YAIR led his people back into the great hall of the palace. From the windows, an eerie orange light cast a flickering glow upon their sullen faces. He waited until they had all entered, and then he spoke.

"My dear friends," he began, "we have spent years together upon this plateau. We have obeyed God's commandments and lived in harmony. Masada was the first fortress to fall into Jewish hands, and now we are the last to survive. In the morning, we will be tested to the fullest, for sunrise brings our final battle.

"I now stand before you and offer you a choice. We can fall into the hands of the Romans and be dragged away as slaves, or we can take our own lives while we are still free people."

Commander Ben Yair looked across the hall at the sea of familiar faces. He could see that many were eager to carry out the deed, but others bowed their heads in fear.

"A man will watch as his wife is pulled away by a group of Roman soldiers. He will hear his children crying, 'Father!' But his hands will be locked in Roman chains.

"Come! We must act now, while our hands are still free to carry a sword. Let us deny the Romans their pleasure and leave them in awe of our death and our courage."

As he looked into his people's faces again, Commander Ben Yair could see that they were no longer afraid.

"Tell us what we must do!" the rabbi called out.

"First," Ben Yair began, "each man must slay his own wife and children."

Like a crackling bolt of lightning, the words exploded in the ears of the people.

"Then the men will return here, write their names on casting lots, and place them in a jar. I will remove ten of these lots. These ten will slay the others. I will then select one last name from the ten remaining lots. This man will slay the other nine, and then himself."

"Now go!" he shouted. "And remember to burn all your personal belongings. We must leave nothing for the Romans!"

Eleazar watched as his people passed silently through the doorway and into the night.

The rabbi began to run as he neared the synagogue. He went straight to the ark and removed the sacred Torah scroll. Lowering it onto the lectern, he softly placed both hands upon it, leaned over, and kissed its cloth cover. Then he raised his head and began scanning the sanctuary.

"I know!" he said to himself as he knelt down and removed several square stone tiles from the floor. He took a small spade from a closet and began digging a hole in the dirt. When he was satisfied that the hole was deep enough, the rabbi returned to the Torah.

He held the scroll in his arms, as he had so many times before. Then the rabbi closed his eyes, silently reciting a prayer, and gently lowered the Torah into the hole.

In the gray light of early morning, column after column of Roman soldiers assembled at the base of the ramp. In perfect symmetry, they marched up the steep incline, halting before the charred remains of the wooden wall. Like one fierce body, they tightly grasped their sharpened

spears. Then a shrill battle cry pierced the air, and they charged in unison through the smoking embers.

Once inside the walls, they were confronted by an eerie stillness and they halted in confusion. They spun around aimlessly, but there was no enemy to be seen.

An old woman walked out through a doorway with her hands above her head.

"Please don't hurt me," she pleaded. "I surrender."

"But where are the others?" a centurion demanded.

Another woman and five children appeared, with frightened looks upon their faces.

"We hid in the cisterns while the others killed themselves," the old woman explained.

"That's ridiculous!" the Roman shouted. "Now, where are they?"

The old woman just lowered her head.

The bewildered soldiers ran past her, fanning out across the top of the plateau. One of them descended a long flight of stairs and walked onto the lower tier of the northern palace. Moments later, his heavy voice echoed through the emptiness.

"Come here quickly!"

Several centurions rushed to his side. Their mouths dropped open and their eyes widened.

Before them, within the soft blanket of morning light, lay a family. A woman's head rested on her husband's shoulder, her long braided hair across his chest. Within their arms was a young boy.

Over the scarred face of Masada, other groups of soldiers were discovering similar scenes. In house after house, they came upon families on the floors of their homes, locked in silent embrace. In the western palace, they discovered scores of bodies lying in rows.

The Romans wandered silently through the courtyards and alley-ways of Masada, with hollow stares upon their faces. For the entire morning, they searched through the fortress. Then they staggered back past spiraling pillars of smoke, over the charred remains of the wooden wall, and retreated down the ramp.

Masada—194 C.E.

W ITH THE FALL OF MASADA, the Romans seized control of the entire country. For many decades, the Jewish population struggled within the iron grip of the empire. But then, in a last bloody rebellion, the Jews rose up and drove the Romans from their shores. Once again, the Romans assembled a great army and returned to crush them.

But this time was to be different. After centuries of turmoil and revolution, the Romans had decided to solve their Jewish problems once and for all. They leveled Jerusalem, and upon the rubble they built a new Roman city called Aelia Capitolina, which the Jews were forbidden to enter. They captured thousands of Jews, enslaved them, and sold them throughout the empire.

Thus, the Jewish people found themselves without a sovereign state. For nearly twenty centuries, they wandered over the face of the earth. Forbidden to own land or dwell among the native populations, they were forced to live in ghettos throughout most of the nations of Europe. Carrying only their memories and traditions, they longed for the day when they would be able to return to their beloved homeland. Each year, at the close of the Passover Seder, Jews around the world would chant, "Next year in Jerusalem."

During these painful times, the land of Israel lay in ruin. For many hundreds of years, a succession of occupiers stripped the country of its forests and natural resources. What remained was an empty wasteland of swamps and deserts. When Mark Twain saw it in 1867, he wrote:

One may ride ten miles, hereabouts, and not see ten human beings. To this region one of the prophecies is applied: "I will bring the land into desolation; and your enemies which dwell therein shall be astonished at it." No man can stand here and say prophecy has not been fulfilled.

Like the rest of Israel, the fortress of Masada lay in ruin. A massive earthquake had reduced the ancient citadel to a pile of broken rock and rubble. Over the years, winter rainstorms slowly eroded the rocks. The relentless desert sun cracked them. Sandstorms covered them over.

As one era followed another, memories of the fabled plateau faded from the pages of history. All that remained were several passages written by the historian Josephus Flavius in the *Bellum Judaicum,* or *The Jewish War,* the seven-volume history of the Roman-Jewish wars that he authored in the first century C.E.

And so the fortress of Masada lay hidden, buried beneath a mountain of debris. It was destined to remain undiscovered and unexplored for many centuries.

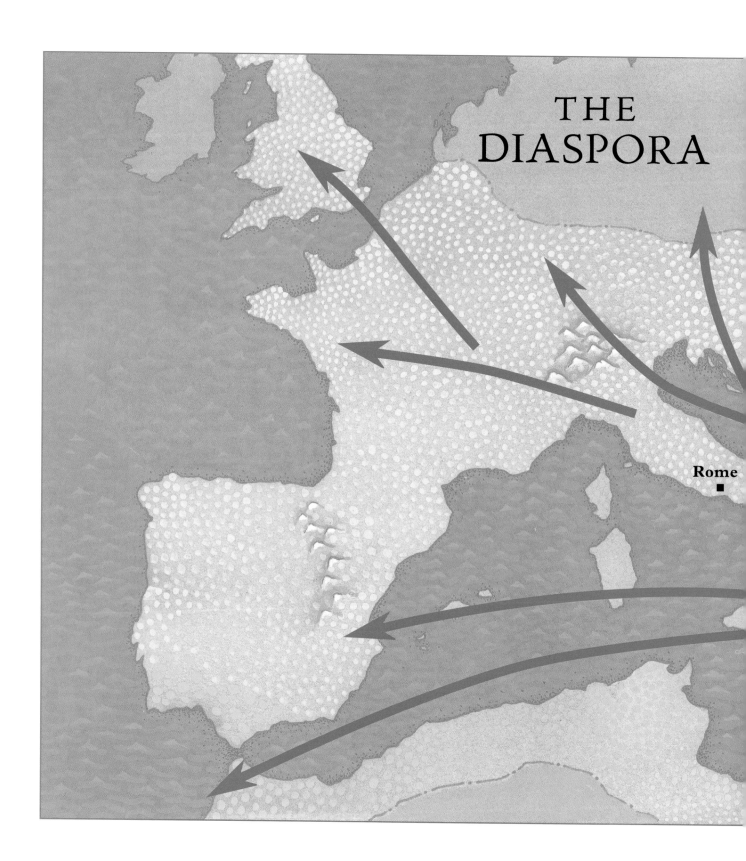

THE
DIASPORA

Rome

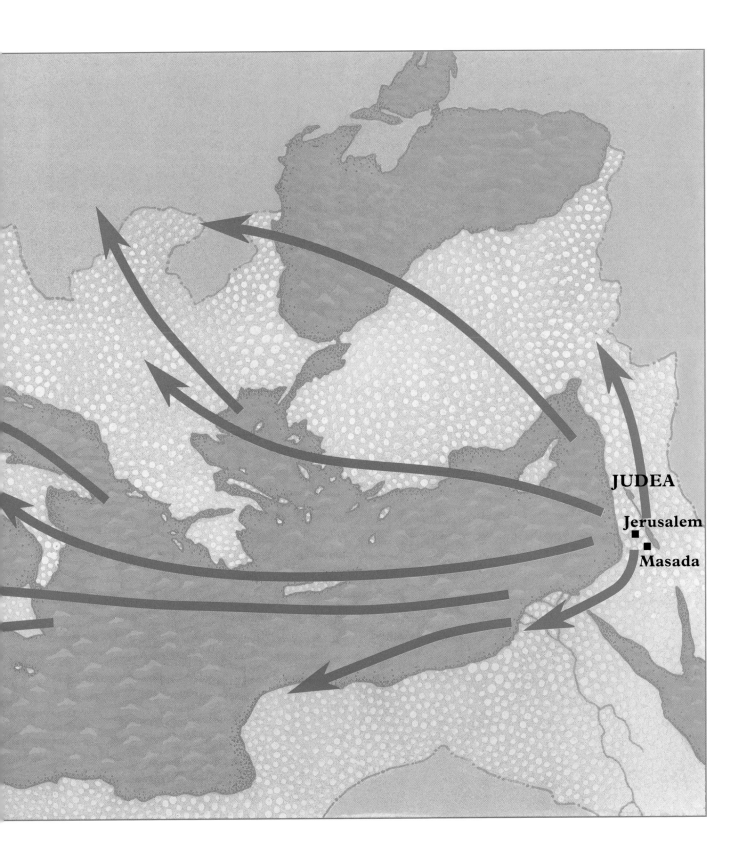

JUDEA

Jerusalem
■
   ■
Masada

Ein Gedi Spring, the Judean Wilderness—1838 C.E.

S THE SUN ROSE over the purple mountains, a long line of camel riders made its way southward through the desert, along the shores of the steaming turquoise sea. Among them were two American scholars, Dr. Edward Robinson and a man known to history only as E. Smith, who had come to survey the geographic features of the Holy Land. The camels climbed a rocky hill and came to rest within a grove of fig and acacia trees. In the middle of the grove was a circular pool of crystal-clear water that bubbled up from between some stones beneath the surface.

The lead rider, a small dark man in flowing white robes, guided his camel down onto its knees and dismounted. He walked from camel to camel, helping the Americans gingerly dismount. They bent over the pool, rinsed their hands and faces, and drank from the cool, sweet waters of the spring. When they had finished, the native guide led the camels to the water's edge.

Dr. Robinson pulled a wooden tripod and a long black telescope from his packs. He was joined by Smith, and together they left the shade of the spring. They slowly made their way to the top of a rocky bluff, where they spread the legs of the tripod and mounted the telescope upon it. As Robinson bent over and peered at the southern horizon, Smith pulled a small leather book from his back pocket. The title was barely visible, etched in worn gold letters—*The Jewish War,* by Josephus Flavius. Smith flipped through the pages, found the passage he sought, and began reading aloud.

"A rock with a very large perimeter and very lofty all the way along is broken off on every side by deep ravines. Their bottom is out of sight, and from it rise sheer cliffs . . . except in two places where the rock can be climbed. One of these comes from the Dead Sea. . . . They call it 'The Snake' because of its narrowness and constant windings. . . ."

Smith stopped reading and stared at a distant plateau among the mountains. Robinson remained bent before the telescope.

"Well, go on!" Robinson demanded at last.

"King Herod devoted great care to the improvement of the place. The entire summit, measuring three-quarters of a mile round, he enclosed within a limestone wall eighteen feet high and twelve feet wide, in which he erected thirty-seven towers, seventy-five feet high. He built a palace too. . . ."

Robinson interrupted suddenly. "I can see the broken walls of a building on the northwestern part of the plateau! And traces of other buildings further east. . . ."

After Robinson and Smith identified the exact location of Masada, other Western scientists and explorers organized expeditions to the ancient fortress. Some were able to make the dangerous climb to the summit, where they discovered the remains of a few broken buildings. Others made detailed surveys of the plateau, and an English artist named Tipping rendered a series of beautiful engravings that helped to publicize the site.

In the last decades of the nineteenth century, the modern Zionist movement was born, and thousands of Jews began returning to the land of Israel. They had suffered through inquisitions, pogroms, and expulsions, never able to find peace in the countries of the Diaspora. Determined to build a modern Jewish nation, they drained malaria-infested swamps, irrigated barren deserts, and built towns, villages, and a totally new kind of cooperative farms called kibbutzim. Groups of young Jews explored the countryside, hiking over mountains and through the wilderness, searching for their roots in the soil of their homeland. Archaeology was their passion, and they unearthed the ancient ruins of many fortresses and cities from the biblical kingdoms of their ancestors.

The story of Masada had special meaning for them. Copies of *The Jewish War* were printed in Hebrew, and many young people were intrigued by several passages that told of a small band of Jewish warriors that had heroically withstood the might of Rome upon an isolated desert outpost. Individually and in groups, they ventured into the desert in search of the ancient citadel.

Shmaryahu Guttman was a founding member of a kibbutz called Na'an in Israel's southern desert. The wild beauty of the region, with its vast expanses and magnificent rock formations, stirred him deeply. He had read *The Jewish War* and was intrigued by the story of the desert fortress.

And so Shmaryahu Guttman decided to hike to Masada. When he reached the summit, he stood for a long time, gazing at the spectacular panorama before him. He looked out across the turquoise waters of the Dead Sea to the distant mountains of Moab. He gazed northward along the shoreline, past the lush oasis of Ein Gedi, and followed the winding dirt road that led to Jericho and Jerusalem.

Guttman turned and studied the rock of the plateau on which he stood. What an amazing geological formation it was! It resembled a colossal table rising up from the desert floor. He wondered if the tale in Josephus's book could be true. He sensed that the answer was buried beneath the rubble that surrounded him.

Yigael Yadin

It was at that moment that Shmaryahu Guttman decided to dedicate his life to the unearthing of the secrets that lay buried within the debris. He began leading groups of young people from his kibbutz to explore Masada's ruins. They climbed the steep cliffs and camped on the flat top of the plateau. Sometimes they remained for a week or two, spending their days searching for clues that would shed light on the dramatic events of Masada's history. Guttman began lobbying to raise funds for an archaeological dig. After many years, the national kibbutz movement agreed to provide them.

Guttman set out with a small team of archaeologists from several kibbutzim. Their finds were dramatic. On the northern tip of the plateau, they discovered the broken remains of the magnificent three-tiered palace of King Herod. They came upon several underground reservoirs and the ruins of an aqueduct that had once fed them. They were the first to map the entire jagged length of the Snake Path, and they partially reconstructed one of the Roman army camps in the valley below. But, most importantly, they captured the imagination of Israel's greatest archaeologist, Yigael Yadin.

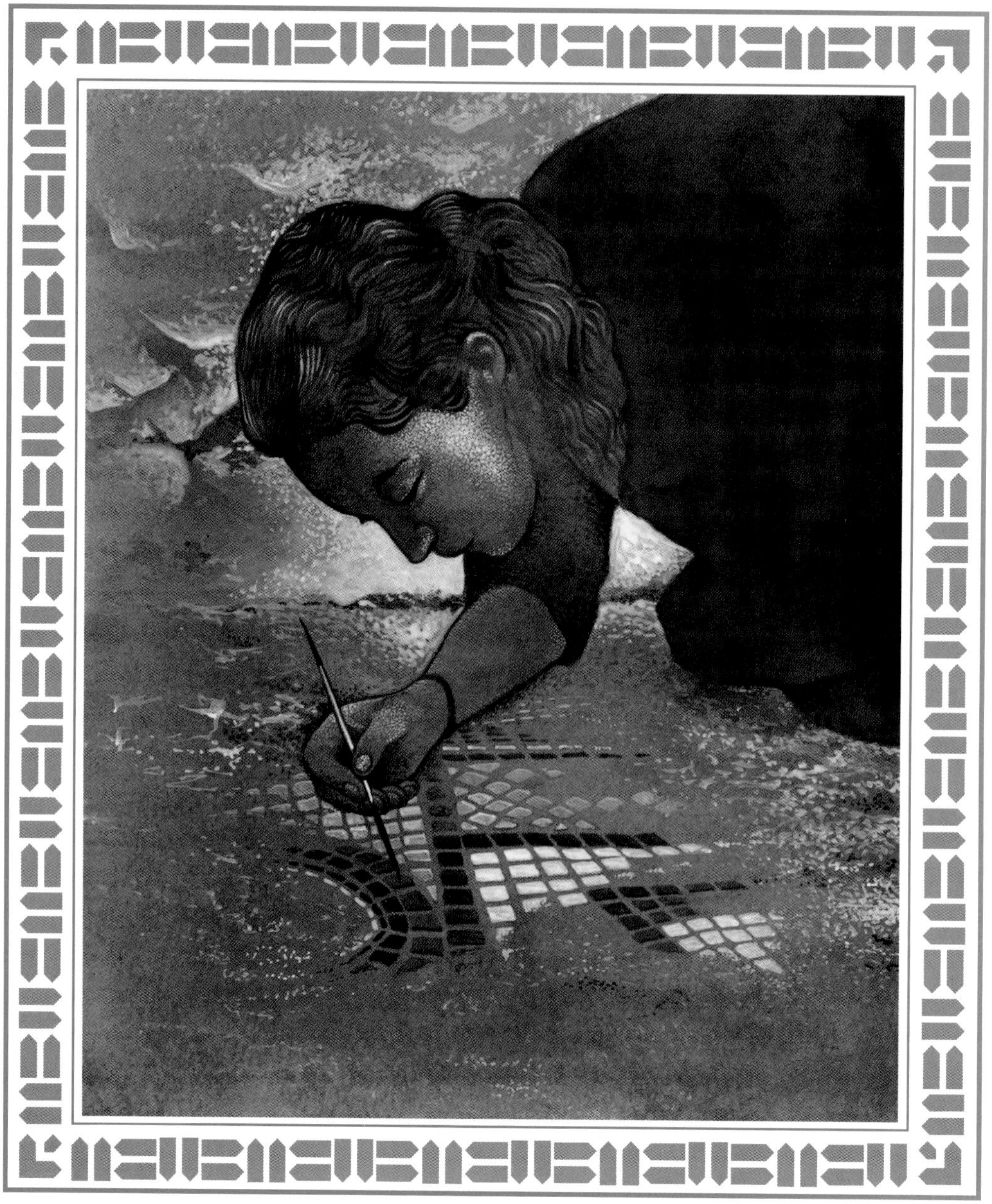

The Negev Desert—1963 C.E.

I N THE OPPRESSIVE HEAT of early afternoon, an army jeep led five buses beyond the outskirts of the sunbaked city of Beersheba. They sped along a modern highway, past endless flatlands of rock and drifting sand. From a distant hillside, a Bedouin boy on a donkey watched as the convoy whizzed by the low black tents of his village. After half an hour, they rounded a sharp curve and began descending toward the Great Rift Valley and the shores of the Dead Sea.

The buses were packed with volunteers from more than twenty nations, who had come to participate in the Masada Archaeological Expedition. It had been organized by the legendary soldier and archaeologist Professor Yigael Yadin.

With the financial support of the Israeli government, the Hebrew University, the Israel Exploration Society, and several private donors, Yadin had assembled a team of renowned archaeologists. One of the team members was an older man with a weather-beaten face and wild tufts of white hair—Shmaryahu Guttman.

The convoy followed the curving road steadily downward, into the forbidding and desolate wilderness of the Great Rift Valley. It slowly descended around hairpin turns, on jagged mountainsides that fell steeply to the shores of the Dead Sea. Within one of the buses, an Israeli guide stood up and faced the volunteers.

"We have now reached the lowest point on the face of the earth," he stated, "twelve hundred feet below sea level. If you look behind us and to the right, you can see the site of the biblical city of Sodom. Notice that the entire area is covered with salt."

The bizarre landscape that surrounded them was straight from the pages of a science-fiction novel. The still green waters looked slick, as if they were actually made of oil. A strange grayish mist rose from the surface, tinting the distant mountains in unearthly hues. Their faded peaks were barely visible, like mirages floating in the purple sky. The coastline was littered with sparkling salt-encrusted stones and white crystalline formations that rose like mushrooms from the water's edge.

The buses continued northward along the sea and then turned inland onto a narrow gravel road that led up into the hills. Within minutes, the sun was hidden by the lofty peaks and the buses came to a stop. One by one, the volunteers stepped out into the barren wilderness. They stood in the shadow of a massive rock. Its sheer cliffs rose, like a great wall, upward into the sky. The Israeli guide turned and pointed toward the top of the precipice.

"There's our destination," he said. "And there's the route we'll take. It's called the Snake Path."

The volunteers stared at the steep zigzagging trail for a long while.

"It looks very dangerous," one of them said.

"Professor Yadin feels that this is the most dramatic way for you to experience Masada for the first time," the guide explained. "We'll take it slowly, and you won't have to make this climb again. Our sleeping quarters are on the opposite side of the plateau. We'll use the Roman ramp from now on. It's a much shorter and easier route."

The guide turned and began his ascent. The volunteers followed in single file. They climbed slowly and carefully, zigzagging back and forth as they rose higher and higher above the desert floor. Every now and then, they stopped to rest and look out at the panorama as it slowly unfolded before them. After about an hour and a half, they reached the summit. They stood still for a while and caught their breath, dazzled by the landscape that was spread far below them like a great map. With feelings of excitement and anticipation, they followed their guide across the plateau and descended on the ancient ramp.

On the following morning, the volunteers quickly climbed to the summit and broke up into three groups. The first group followed their leader toward a huge pile of rubble on the western side of the plateau. They began carefully sifting through the debris, examining every fragment for the possible clues it might reveal. They soon began uncovering scores of round stones about the size of grapefruits. As they dug deeper, they came upon hundreds of them. It was their first major discovery, for these were the very stones that the Romans had launched from the assault tower during the final days of the siege.

On the northern tip of the plateau, a second team of diggers unearthed several broken columns and cracked wall paintings on the lower tier of King Herod's palace. As they dug further, they came upon some bronze arrows, bits of clothing, and a woman's sandal. They unearthed a small bathing pool, and upon its smooth white surface they found a large dark stain that appeared to be blood. Beside the pool were the skeletons of three people: a young man and woman and a boy. The woman's dark braided hair was amazingly intact, preserved for nearly two thousand years in the arid air of the desert.

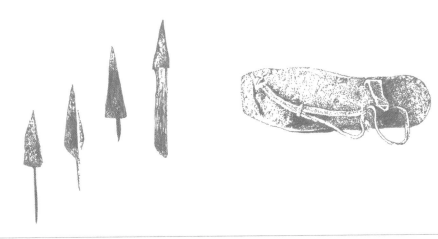

The third team discovered three smaller palaces with beautiful mosaic floors, fluted stone columns, and murals on the walls. Within these buildings were crude stone walls dividing the interior space into many small rooms. These were the Zealots' modest homes.

Within these simple dwellings, the volunteers came upon the most touching of discoveries. For in the corner of many rooms lay a pile of ashes containing the burned personal belongings of a family. Josephus had written that, before taking their own lives, the Zealots set fire to their meager possessions so they wouldn't fall into Roman hands.

The diggers came upon an unusual square building on the north-western edge of the plateau. As they removed the rubble, they uncovered four rows of stone benches along the walls. This was clearly some sort of Zealot meeting hall. But what could its use have been? Professor Yadin reasoned that they might have unearthed the Zealots' synagogue. Throughout Israel, there was much excitement, for a synagogue this ancient had never before been discovered. When a small piece of parchment with the words *priestly tithe* written on it was found upon the floor, Yadin began to believe that his hunch had been correct.

Then Yadin had an exciting thought: If *he* had been the rabbi of the synagogue, he wouldn't have allowed the Romans to discover the sacred Torah scroll. But neither would he have been permitted to destroy it. And so, Yadin deduced, the rabbi must have hidden it! The diggers were directed to remove the stone tiles upon the floor, and there, buried in the dirt, was the oldest Torah scroll ever to have been found.

Many finds on Masada were on a grand scale. Palaces and villas were unearthed, revealing the wealth and opulence of ancient Rome. But occasionally, the discovery of a tiny fragment could be equally telling. Within a pile of rubble near the synagogue, a small piece of glass was discovered. It was slightly curved and probably part of some sort of bottle. Upon the fragment was an ancient inscription that was still perfectly legible—*To King Herod of Judea.* It had once held wine from King Herod's royal cellars, shipped to Masada from the vineyards of Italy.

There were many other wonderful finds at Masada—a classic Roman bathhouse, a cluster of storerooms where dried food and weapons were kept, the casemate defense wall, and a public swimming pool. The volunteers also uncovered hundreds of ancient coins from the five years of Jewish independence following the revolt against Rome, fragments from a wide variety of ancient scrolls, and enough pottery to fill a museum.

Among these fragments were several small clay casting lots with Zealots' names scrawled upon them in ancient Hebrew. One of them bears the name Ben Yair.

The dramatic story of Masada has been passed down through the generations for nearly two thousand years, thanks to the writings of Josephus Flavius. His account is the only written record that survived through the centuries.

It was Josephus's tale that inspired adventurers, explorers, and dreamers to venture out into the desert in search of the lost citadel. And when the fortress of Masada was finally discovered by the American Dr. Edward Robinson, it was Josephus's physical description of the plateau that served as Robinson's guide.

Until that time, many scholars had dismissed Josephus's story as romanticized fancy. After all, a story so wild and improbable could never have really happened. It was a tall tale, a myth, reading more like an adventure story than a piece of history.

But when archaeologists began digging through the rubble atop the plateau, they unearthed a wide array of artifacts that exactly matched the descriptions of Josephus. And when Yigael Yadin's full-scale excavation was completed, virtually all of Josephus's story was verified.

Still, there are skeptics who continue to insist that Josephus's story must be fictional. Some claim that since suicide is against Jewish law, the Zealots of Masada would never have taken their own lives. Others argue that the archaeological evidence is inconclusive, because the physical remains of most of the Zealots were never found. Still others contend that Josephus is an unreliable source, because the purpose of his books was to justify his own life and glorify Rome.

In writing this book, I have chosen to tell the story as if it happened exactly as Josephus describes it. All of the named characters were real people, though most of the dialogue was created to dramatize the tale.

B.C.E.

- 39 Herod crowned King of Judea
- 37 Herod's marriage to Mariamme
- 29 Murder of Mariamme
- 23 Rebuilding of Solomon's Temple in Jerusalem
- 6 Birth of Jesus
- 4 Death of Herod

C.E.

- 33 Crucifixion of Jesus
- 37 Birth of Josephus
- 54 Accession of Nero as emperor of Rome
- 66 Florus's attack in Jerusalem
  Masada captured by Sicarii
  Outbreak of war
- 67 Arrival in Galilee of Vespasian and Titus
  Surrender of Josephus at Jotapata
  Fall of most of Galilee
- 68 Fall of most of Judea
  Death of Nero
- 69 Vespasian proclaimed emperor while in Egypt
- 70 Vespasian returns to Rome
  Siege of Jerusalem begun (spring)
  Circumvallation wall built around Jerusalem
  Holy Temple in Jerusalem burned (autumn)
  Triumphal procession in Rome
- 71 Capture of Herodion and Machaerus
- 73 Fall of Masada
- 75 Josephus completes the *Bellum Judaicum,* or *The Jewish War*
- 131 Last revolt against Rome
- 135 Total destruction of Jerusalem
  Construction of a new city called Aelia Capitolina
  Exile of the Jews
- 1838 Discovery of Masada by Robinson and Smith
- 1881 Jews begin returning to Israel
- 1948 Birth of the modern state of Israel
- 1953 Guttman expedition
- 1963 Yadin expedition begun
- 1965 Yadin expedition completed

Aqueduct: A bridgelike structure made of stone, widely used by the Romans for carrying water across a valley or over a river.

Assault tower: A Roman war machine, made of wood covered by iron plates or animal skins, that could be rolled up to a defense wall in order to attack it. Archers stationed at the top provided efficient covering fire directed against enemy defenders.

Battering ram: A huge timber sheathed in iron, swung like a pendulum from a wooden framework. Battering rams were sometimes as long as one hundred feet and worked by as many as two hundred men. They were capable of breaking down almost any wall.

Bedouin: An Arab from the deserts of southwest Asia and North Africa, traditionally tent dwelling and depending on animal herds for subsistence.

Casemate wall: A thick, hollow defense wall, usually surrounding a city or fortress, containing soldiers' barracks within.

Casting lots: A set of objects drawn from a container to decide a question by chance.

Catapult: An ancient military engine for hurling stones, arrows, and spears.

Centurion: A Roman army soldier.

Circumvallation: A wall or ditch built beyond the outskirts of a fortification, used by the Romans to prevent enemy soldiers from escaping.

Cistern: An underground reservoir for storing water.

Dead Sea: A salt lake between the modern states of Israel and Jordan. The lowest lake in the world, 390 square miles, 1,293 feet below sea level.

Diaspora: The scattering of the Jews to countries outside of Israel, first by the Babylonians and then by the Romans.

Forum: In ancient Rome, the center of judicial and business affairs, a large public place of assembly.

Galilee: An ancient Roman province within the land of Israel, north of Judea between the Sea of Galilee and the Mediterranean coast.

Inquisition: A Catholic tribunal engaged chiefly in combating heresy. In 1492, it ordered the expulsion of the entire Jewish population from Spain.

Israel: The northern kingdom of the ancient Hebrews, including ten of the twelve tribes. In modern times, a Jewish state created in 1948, covering 7,984 square miles, with the capital city of Jerusalem.

Judea: The southern region of ancient Israel that existed under Persian, Greek, and Roman rule.

Judean wilderness: An arid region in Judea, south of Jerusalem, on the western shores of the Dead Sea.

Jupiter: The supreme deity of the ancient Romans, associated with sky and rain.

Kibbutz (plural: kibbutzim): An Israeli agricultural settlement where all labor is done collectively and profits are shared equally among its members. Originally established early in the twentieth century by young idealists from Russia and Eastern Europe in an attempt to create a utopian society.

Legion: The largest unit of the Roman army, comprising four to six thousand foot soldiers with a much smaller complement of cavalry.

Menorah: A traditional oil lamp or candle holder with seven branches used in the Holy Temple in Jerusalem and decoratively placed in modern synagogues.

Moab: An ancient kingdom, east of the Dead Sea, in what is now Jordan.

Pogroms: Organized massacres of the Jewish populations of Russia and Eastern Europe, beginning around 1880, carried out by the armies of those countries.

Portico of Octavia: A large structure in ancient Rome consisting of a roof supported by rows of columns and dedicated to Octavia, the wife of Marc Antony and sister of Augustus.

Rabbi: A Jewish scholar qualified to rule on questions of Jewish law. In the first century C.E., rabbis usually performed their religious functions on a part-time basis, while working in their primary occupations most of the time.

Rampart: A thick defense wall surrounding many ancient cities.

Ram's horn: The hollow horn of a ram used as a trumpet in ancient times for both religious and military purposes.

Sicarii: A splinter group of Zealots. Their name means "Daggermen," from the Latin *sica,* meaning "dagger." Their violent methods before and during the revolt against Rome struck fear in the hearts of Jews and Romans alike.

Siege: The act of surrounding, sealing off, and attacking a fortified place in order to compel the surrender of its defenders. The Romans were the masters of siege warfare. They created a sophisticated array of machines, weapons, and strategies for breaking through a fortification's walls.

Tableau: A group of people, costumed and motionless within a stage set, representing a particular scene or event.

Tithe: A tenth portion of goods or income, paid as tax to the synagogue.

Torah scroll: The Five Books of Moses, the first five books of the Bible, written by scribes on parchment and read during services at a synagogue.

Valley of Kidron: A ravine on the east side of Jerusalem that is a traditional site of judgment.

Wadi: A dry streambed common in the Middle East.

Zealot: The main war party in Galilee and Judea during the revolt against Rome. Their self-chosen name was derived from their watchword: *No God but Yahweh, no tax but to the Temple, no friend but the Zealot.*

Bibliography

Cornfeld, Gaalyah. *This Is Masada.* New York: Scribner, 1967.

Flavius, Josephus. *The Jewish War.* New York: Penguin, 1981.

Grant, M. *The Jews in the Roman World.* London: Weidenfeld & Nicolson, 1973.

Sachar, Abram Leon. *A History of the Jews.* New York: Knopf, 1968.

Smallwood, Mary. *The Jews under Roman Rule.* Kinderhook, NY: E. J. Brill, 1976.

Yadin, Yigael. *Masada.* New York: Random House, 1966.

Art Notes

These illustrations were taken from the following sources:

Title page: A Roman coin commemorating the fall of Jerusalem, 70 C.E.

Page 2: Coins minted in Jerusalem during the five years of Jewish independence, 66–70 C.E.

Pages 14, 20, and 21: Roman statues.

Page 18: A relief sculpture of Jewish slaves on the Arch of Titus in Rome.

Page 30: A relief sculpture of Roman centurions.

Page 40: A relief sculpture of Romans executing prisoners of war.

Page 51: An Israeli army photograph of Yigael Yadin.

Pages 55, 57, 61, and 64: Artifacts found at Masada.

Page 58: A photograph of Masada after the Yadin excavation.

Page 60: A contemporary Israeli medallion.

Index